ROAD SIGNS
ON THE
JOURNEY HOME

FIFTY-TWO MODERN-DAY PROVERBS

BERNIE BROWN

Inspiring Voices®
A Service of **Guideposts**

Copyright © 2014 Bernie Brown.

All rights reserved. No part of this book may be used or reproduced by any means, graphic, electronic, or mechanical, including photocopying, recording, taping or by any information storage retrieval system without the written permission of the publisher except in the case of brief quotations embodied in critical articles and reviews.

Scriptures taken from the Holy Bible, New International Version®, NIV®. Copyright © 1973, 1978, 1984, 2011 by Biblica, Inc.™ Used by permission of Zondervan. All rights reserved worldwide. www.zondervan.com The "NIV" and "New International Version" are trademarks registered in the United States Patent and Trademark Office by Biblica, Inc.™ All rights reserved.

Inspiring Voices books may be ordered through booksellers or by contacting:

Inspiring Voices
1663 Liberty Drive
Bloomington, IN 47403
www.inspiringvoices.com
1 (866) 697-5313

Because of the dynamic nature of the Internet, any web addresses or links contained in this book may have changed since publication and may no longer be valid. The views expressed in this work are solely those of the author and do not necessarily reflect the views of the publisher, and the publisher hereby disclaims any responsibility for them.

Any people depicted in stock imagery provided by Thinkstock are models, and such images are being used for illustrative purposes only. Certain stock imagery © Thinkstock.

ISBN: 978-1-4624-0922-8 (sc)
ISBN: 978-1-4624-0923-5 (e)

Library of Congress Control Number: 2014904321

Printed in the United States of America.

Inspiring Voices rev. date: 03/13/2014

To the transportation and highway
departments throughout our country,
who place road signs on our streets, highways, and roadways
that lead to our earthly homes, and to the
Holy Spirit, who guides our paths
on our journeys to our
heavenly home

CONTENTS

Foreword xi
Preface xiii
Appreciation xv
Introduction xvii

Road Signs: Modern-Day Proverbs 1
   1.   My Daddy Works Here 3
   2.   Stop 5
   3.   Yield 7
   4.   Railroad Crossing 9
   5.   Work Zone 11
   6.   Rest Area 13
   7.   Crossroads 15
   8.   Speed Limit 17
   9.   Detour 19
  10.   One-Lane Bridge 21
  11.   One Way 23
  12.   Truck Route 25
  13.   Do Not Enter 27
  14.   Speed Bump 29
  15.   No U-Turn 31
  16.   No Horn Blowing 33
  17.   Bridge Ices before Road 35
  18.   Low and Soft Shoulder 37

19.	Narrow Bridge Ahead	39
20.	Call Box	41
21.	Click It or Ticket	43
22.	Uneven Pavement	45
23.	No Parking	47
24.	Deer Crossing	49
25.	Rock Slides	51
26.	Keep Off the Median	53
27.	Fog Area	55
28.	Weigh Station	57
29.	Runaway Truck Ramp	59
30.	Winding Road	61
31.	Fire Station	63
32.	Handicap Parking	65
33.	Share the Road	67
34.	Toll Road	69
35.	Historical District	71
36.	Photo Enforced	73
37.	School	75
38.	Adopt a Highway	77
39.	Roundabout	79
40.	No Throwing Trash	81
41.	Tunnel	83
42.	They Kill (DUI) Don't Do It	85
43.	Church	87
44.	Lights on When Raining	89
45.	Terrapin Xing	91
46.	Evacuation Route	93
47.	Scenic View	95
48.	Destination and Distance	97
49.	City Limit	99

50. No Outlet	101
51. Slow Grandparents at Play	103
52. Hospital	105
Home	107

Bonus: A Few Other Messages	109
Reflections and Conclusions	113
Epilogue: Photography Experiences	117
Study Guide	121
Study Guide Form	123

FOREWORD

Once again Bernie Brown has taken a uniquely creative look at an ordinary situation and offered profound insight into underlying truths. Those of us who are familiar with his other works are not at all surprised. After all, he took a simple motto *("Professionally We Serve, Personally We Care")* to inspire the work force of one of the largest healthcare organizations in the country. He used a simple *"Yield"* sign to offer a new glimpse into servant leadership, and he took a line from an old ballad *("Frankie and Johnnie were sweethearts")* to provide a view into his own creative and loving marriage.

In this new work, Bernie is prepared to take us on a ride, but he has not chosen "a road less traveled." Instead, this is the road that we travel every day—through the countryside, down the freeway, to the office, to school, to the grocery store. It involves the road signs encountered along the way that we often dismiss. Bernie uses those simple signs to grab our attention, to express his own faith and core values, and to encourage us to learn something about ourselves and God's claim on our lives.

This is neither a drive-by book nor is it to be considered flippantly. It is not for the casual passer-by and not a ninety-mile rush through the journey. Instead, it's for the one who wants a contemplative look into his/her faith with an experienced churchman, a dedicated husband and father, an accomplished business leader, and an all-round good guy.

Now grab your hat and coat. Watch the road! Bernie will take you on a ride that can change your life.

--Dr. Sam R. Matthews, Senior Minister
First United Methodist Church, Marietta, GA

****

Bernie Brown has given us a gift! In his distinctive, affable, winsome, South Georgia style he has imaginatively taken something out of everyday living and given it wings. Who could have ever so creatively considered how a road sign speaks to the human heart … but Bernie did. He takes a common piece of life and living and makes it come alive.

As you pour through these pages, you will be awestruck at the common sense, hope-filled spirituality that he places before us to digest. You'll be amazed at the richness of the language, the impact of the instruction, and the poignancy of the message. It is Bernie Brown at his finest. Well, more than that, it is the God of Bernie Brown resourcefully taking us to a place where enlargement of our soul occurs.

Reader beware! If you take to heart the pages you are about to experience, you will undoubtedly find the winds of transformation blowing through your life. Moreover, you will never, ever look at a road sign again without thinking of the way of Jesus and a remarkable Jesus-following servant named Bernie.

Thank you, Bernie, for the gift!

--Dr. Charles (Chuck) W. Wilson II, Senior Pastor
Long's Chapel United Methodist Church, Lake Junaluska, NC

Bernie and Snookie Brown have been members of Marietta First UMC for forty three years and affiliate members of Long's Chapel UMC for twelve years.

PREFACE

Several of my friends have asked me, "How did you come up with the crazy idea of observing road signs?" I honestly can't remember what enticed me to begin this unusual but fascinating journey. However, in retrospect, I do recall one incident that may have prompted my inquiry. And as Snookie, my wife, always says, "It wasn't a coincidence. It was a God-incidence!"

Several years ago, we were taking a scenic drive with friends on I-40 up in the mountains of western North Carolina. I noticed a state trooper pull out as we passed a ramp. I was not going too fast, but to be safe, I set the cruise control on sixty-four miles per hour, just below the limit. He followed us for about five miles, and then I saw and heard what all drivers dread: flashing lights and a blaring siren. My first thought was that my rear lights weren't working; I knew that my license tag was current. I stopped and had to wait a few minutes before the trooper came up to the car. I'm sure he was first checking me out on his computer. Snookie and our friends didn't say a word, and my face was flushed with fear and embarrassment.

After Sergeant Valentine introduced himself and asked for my license and registration, I proceeded to plead innocent to every possible traffic infraction. I even pointed out that I knew that he was following so I was doubly cautious and placed my cruise control on sixty-four miles per hour to make certain I wouldn't exceed the speed limit.

After listening patiently, he informed me that the speed limit up in the mountains was fifty-five and that going around curves above that speed would be very dangerous. Then, in an authoritative, stern voice, he said something I remember to this day: "Mr. Brown, the state of North Carolina has spent millions of dollars to place signs along our roads to get you home safely. In the future, I would appreciate it if you would pay attention to them and act accordingly." As he handed me the ticket, he said, "Have a good day." Across the piece of paper was written the word *Warning*. And, sure enough, as we returned home, I noticed the fifty-five miles per hour speed-limit signs on that stretch of winding mountain highway.

If there was a beginning point for my interest in road signs, it probably was that day. And what I remember most was the officer's directive: "Pay attention to them and act accordingly."

APPRECIATION

A special thanks to those who have assisted in obtaining the photographs of road signs that inspired the messages included in this work. In this effort, my wife, Snookie, was a trooper, as always. She took the majority of the photos, bravely standing on roadways in four different states during this past year. Some other new friends who provided several of the unusual and hard-to-find signs include Stuntman Stu (*My Daddy Works Here*), Cory Doctorow (*No Horn Blowing*), the freephotooftheday website (*Rock Slides*), Roy Schreffler (*Fog Area*), and Peter Ubriaco (*Toll Road*).

I would like to express my deep appreciation to my two senior pastors, Dr. Sam Matthews (Marietta First United Methodist Church) and Dr. Chuck Wilson (Long's Chapel United Methodist Church), who have given their encouragement and support, and were kind enough to write the foreword for the book.

I also offer a special thank-you to the Inspiring Voices team for their expertise and support on this unique project—my fourth book published by them.

INTRODUCTION

If someone asked me to name my most favorite place, without hesitation I would answer, "Home." As a kid, I liked going places, but I loved coming home. I've had fifteen different addresses so far; therefore, many roads in many towns and states have been on my routes home. Today, I can think of nothing more satisfying than to go home to be with my very best friend: my wife. Therefore, the roads that lead home are the ones I cherish.

When we travel now, I usually do the driving because I suffer from motion sickness. Being behind the steering wheel requires continuous concentration and awareness, so I'm generally the one who notices things like billboards and signs along the way. Road signs have several characteristics that stand out to me. They have few words and sometimes just symbols that convey important messages quickly; they are different colors and shapes, which makes each of them instantly recognizable; and they are in places where immediate instruction and guidance are needed.

One day it occurred to me how vital road signs are to us. As we travel from place to place—and particularly back home after a long day, a long trip, a late meeting, and the like—road signs are our friends. They alert us to potential danger; they remind us where we are and how far we have to go; they help direct steering and speed; they assist in our staying on course. Through these and other means, they contribute to our arrival home safe and sound. Adherence to their guidance along our journey is crucial.

Could road signs also be helpful to us on another journey? I believe that these instructional aids may be even more important on a different one that we all will make: our life journey toward our eternal home. The roadways on this journey may be even more challenging and certainly more vital. We seem to be traveling constantly at high speeds with poor visibility on crowded roads. The lifestyles in our society today are fraught with danger and uncertainty. Therefore, let's look at road signs from this different perspective and see what guidance they can give us.

I have selected fifty-two signs that I have observed on my travels for more than seventy years and in this book share the message and life lessons I received from each of them. Of course, many signs carry similar messages, so I've attempted to choose a representative sample. They are not arranged in any particular order; as on the roadways, they are placed only where there is a need.

Therefore, I hope and pray these will meet you at your point of need when you read them. My suggestion is that you focus on one sign at a time, and I also challenge you to identify additional road signs that are not included here but offer direction and guidance. As we explore these together, I believe that you will agree; they are truly our friends.

I enjoy the book of Proverbs in the Old Testament of the Bible. It helps me view things from a broader and deeper perspective by differentiating wisdom from mere knowledge. The word proverb, when broken down, means *pro*—being for something, an affirmation, and *verb*—expressing an act. It calls for positive action or response. A proverb by definition is a popular maxim or an adage. It's common talk that is understandable and instructional, giving wise counsel in regard to the art of living. I contend that road signs share many of the very same attributes. Therefore, I offer to you my reflections about these as *modern-day proverbs*. It is amazing how the right message delivered at the appropriate time gives the needed direction as we travel home. So hop in, and let's head out together on a fascinating journey of discovery.

> *"So your trust may be in the Lord, I teach you today, even you. Have I not written excellent sayings for you, sayings of counsel and knowledge, teaching you true and reliable words so that you can give sound answers to him who sent you?" Proverbs 22:19–21*

ROAD SIGNS: MODERN-DAY PROVERBS

As you view the following road signs, I suggest that you give them more than just a glance. In merely looking *at* them, you will be using your gift of *sight*; but to look *into their purpose* allows you to exercise your gift of *insight*. The goal here is to discover deeper meanings that offer lessons for life's journeys. Perhaps the lessons we gain will serve us well, much like those from the book of Proverbs.

"It really worked on me."

1
MY DADDY WORKS HERE

"Listen, my son, to your father's instruction."
Proverbs 1:8

THIS PARTICULAR ROAD SIGN, first spotted on the way home from an out-of-state trip, moved me emotionally more than any had in the past. It was beside the highway just as we entered a major work zone lasting for more than ten miles. Of course, its intent was to, in a very personal manner, heighten drivers' consciousness of the need to slow down and be especially aware and careful in that area. It really worked on me. I don't ever remember being so mindful of a work zone; I observed all the workers and equipment along that particular stretch of roadway. As we were leaving the zone, I realized I had seen a similar message before. But instead of being on a road sign saying, *"Please Slow Down, My Daddy Works Here,"* it was in a book that read, "Be still and know that I am God, [your Father who's at work here]" (Palm 46:10). That really worked on me too.

Dear Lord,
On our journey, may we never forget that all the roads carrying us home are continual work zones. Remind us to slow down and marvel at your great handiwork that's still in progress. And please work on us. Amen.

"...it means stop!"

2
STOP

"Blessed is he who keeps the law".
Proverbs 29:18

ON THE WAY TO and from work each day, I used to save time by cutting through a neighborhood with little traffic. On one occasion in the early evening as I approached a familiar intersection, I just slowed down and proceeded through it despite an obvious *Stop* sign. Unfortunately for me, a local police car stationed just out of my view witnessed this and promptly gave chase with full lights and siren blazing. Of course, it was more than embarrassing to have a few friends wave as they passed and observed me in this compromised position. My defense was that I could see in both directions, and I had slowed down. His response to me before issuing a stern warning (thank goodness he was benevolent that time) was, "A stop sign doesn't mean slow down; it means stop!" I believe there are more stop signs on our roadways than any other kind of sign. There must be a reason for this.

Dear Lord,

Help us to remember that stop means stop. You have placed stop signs along our way to warn us of danger and to remind us that others also are traveling along the same roads. Thank you especially for this road sign that can keep us from crashing. Amen.

"…allows judgment to be exercised."

3
YIELD

"If you are wise, your wisdom will reward you."
Proverbs 9:12

UNLIKE THE STOP SIGN, which is definitive in nature, the *Yield* sign allows judgment to be exercised. If there is no traffic or danger at an intersection, a driver need not come to an absolute stop but can proceed with caution. We have been equipped to use discretion in many areas of our lives. But in having multiple choices, we need to remember that while we must yield to avoid pending danger, there are also times when we should not yield to such things as temptation. Interestingly, the word *yield* has two definitions: to surrender and to produce. Maybe there is a connection here.

Dear Lord,
As we make choices in this complicated game called life, please give us wisdom and discernment to make the right ones. Help us recognize danger and those things that will do us harm and cause separation from you. Also, teach us to yield (surrender) our will to you so we can abundantly yield (produce) fruit for the kingdom. Amen.

"Panic was my first reaction."

4
RAILROAD CROSSING

"A prudent man sees danger."
Proverbs 22:2

FOR MORE THAN FIFTY years, we have enjoyed a quarterly fishing trip in south Georgia. It was dark as we returned to the lake cabin from dinner at a local restaurant one night. On that country road is an old *Railroad Crossing* sign, but no lights that blink or arms that come down to stop traffic. In all those years, we had never seen a train cross the road; actually, I thought the tracks were inactive. Like in the past, I slowed down slightly to absorb the bump. Then an unexpected and harrowing thing happened: a large moving object was coming toward us. Panic was my first reaction, but fortunately the freight train was not yet at full throttle. I pressed the pedal that propelled us across the tracks about twenty seconds before the train crossed the road. I learned that day that complacency and a false sense of security can result in a train wreck.

Dear Lord,
Please help us to be alert to the real dangers that cross our paths. Some of these can be as large as a freight train. Amen.

"...*fines are doubled.*"

5
WORK ZONE

"Whoever gives heed to instruction prospers, and blessed is he who trusts in the Lord."
Proverbs 16:20

THERE IS A STRETCH of I-75 from the northern to the southern borders of our state that I have been traveling for many years. I can't remember a single trip when some part of this busy interstate highway was not being repaired, expanded, or modified in some way. It has constantly been adorned with *Work Zone* signs. Almost everyone becomes irritated because of the inconvenience and delays this causes. But what if our roads were allowed to deteriorate and become even more crowded? What if we were still riding on this major highway as constructed in the 1960s? Despite our initial reaction, inconvenience and delays many times can improve our lives. It goes without saying: this is a time to slow down—fines are doubled.

Dear Lord,
Help us to recognize that we live in a world that is not finished and is constantly under repair and modification. Give us the wisdom to identify and support constructive improvement in the work zones of our lives. Amen.

"…I feel renewed and invigorated…"

6
REST AREA

"Then you can go on your way in safety,
and your foot will not stumble."
Proverbs 3:23

STRATEGICALLY LOCATED ALONG MAJOR highways are *Rest Areas*. Often they are at the state line and serve as welcome centers, and other times they are between major cities on isolated stretches of road. Irrespective of their location, they serve a useful purpose. We stop at a rest area often to get out and move our cramped limbs, use the restrooms, have a short lunch, or just swap drivers. I don't know that we really rest, but each time I feel renewed and invigorated to finish the journey. Now when making a long trip, we have begun to locate rest area symbols on the map in anticipation of these important sources of respite.

Dear Lord,

Help us to recognize the fact that periodically we need a break. May we remember that you designated both a time and a place for rest and renewal—Sunday and church! Amen.

"…choose the correct road…"

7
CROSSROADS

"Make level paths for your feet and take only ways that are firm."
Proverbs 4:26

OUR HIGHWAYS ARE FILLED with intersections where two or more roads cross. If we are in unfamiliar territory, these junctions can be confusing and challenging. It's also crucial to remember the old adage "If we don't know where we are going, any road will lead us there." The great American philosopher Yogi Berra once said, "When you come to a fork in the road, take it." Of course, this is impossible; *Crossroads* call for decisions on our part. If we view this in the context of our life's journey, we must choose the correct road that leads us home, so it is very important that we know where our ultimate home is.

Dear Lord,
*   We look forward to our homecoming someday. Help us to make the right decisions when we come to the many crossroads in life. Give us the wisdom to select the road that leads home. Amen.*

"…there are behavioral boundaries…"

8
SPEED LIMIT

"Do not move an ancient boundary set up by your forefathers."
Proverbs 22:28

IF YOU TRAVEL ON interstate highways, you notice that *Speed Limit* signs appear often. On the high side, the limit usually varies from fifty-five to seventy miles per hour. Interestingly, there often is also a minimum speed required: forty or fifty. (You may know the story about the little old lady who told the patrolman who pulled her over for going only twenty-five, "I know why you stopped me. I was the only one you could catch.") Of course, in populated and congested areas, limits are much lower. It should be no surprise that more citations and fines are bestowed on drivers for speeding than for any other traffic infraction. I admit, probably like you, that this is one area in which I must plead guilty from time to time. However, the point here is that there are behavioral boundaries that are set for our own good.

Dear Lord,
Help us not to speed through our lives and harm others or ourselves. Please guide our pace so we arrive home just when you expect us. Amen.

"…it is what it is…"

9
DETOUR

"He who obeys instructions guards his life, but he who is contemptuous of his ways will die."
Proverbs 19:16

I WAS ON MY way to a much-anticipated meeting with my buddies at our favorite fishing hole. When I had less than five miles to go, a *Detour* sign appeared in the middle of the road with an arrow pointing to an alternate, but much longer, route to the lake. I could see the bridge up ahead, which had been damaged by flooding. Detours can interrupt our journeys—some at very inopportune times. In response, we have choices: we can either become upset and bitter, or we can accept that it is what it is and follow the detour signs to our ultimate destination. On this particular occasion, I arrived about twenty minutes late, but I felt even more enthusiastic and excited because I had a bit more time to anticipate a wonderful experience.

Dear Lord,
When detours interrupt our journey, please give us patience, perseverance, and peace. Help us to realize that delays are only temporary and that a safe, late arrival home can be sweeter than ever. Amen.

"...take turns proceeding across..."

10
ONE-LANE BRIDGE

"A cheerful look brings joy to the heart."
Proverbs 15:30

I REMEMBER A FEW one-lane bridges from when I was growing up, but I know of only one in our area that still exists. It's the one-lane bridge across the dam at Lake Junaluska, North Carolina. The term "one lane" in this case simply means the bridge is so narrow, it can accommodate cars going only one way at a time. Therefore, a system has been devised to alternate the flow of traffic: cars approaching from different directions take turns proceeding across the bridge. This particular crossing is fascinating; off to one side is the lake and on the other is the waterfall from the dam, which forms a large stream at the bottom. At the entrance to each end, there is the sign *One Lane Bridge, Please be Courteous.* I have crossed it many times and not once observed anyone discourteous or angry. To the contrary, in most cases, drivers wave to each other as they wait their turn. It is amazing how a little sign can not only encourage folks to be nice to each other but also make them feel better about themselves.

Dear Lord,

It is encouraging to see people cooperating with each other, instead of the usual bickering that seems to be the new norm. Please help us add this little phrase at the end of all the signs that guide us on our journey: please be courteous. Amen.

"…on a one way street going the wrong way."

11
ONE WAY

"Stern discipline awaits him who leaves the path."
Proverbs 15:10

IN SAVANNAH, GEORGIA, WHERE I once lived, the streets in the downtown district have an interesting pattern. Between the main streets that circle a series of squares, there are *One-way* streets. These alternately go in difference directions. So, for a scenic drive, you follow the main ones around the beautiful squares, but if you are in a hurry, you take the one-way streets. For those who have never been to this fascinating, historic city, this can be confusing. Unless you pay attention, you can easily find yourself on a one-way street going the wrong way. However, for the natives, this all works very well. Many times in our life journey, we need to go slowly and enjoy the scenery, but on other occasions we need to get somewhere in a hurry. In this regard, one-way streets serve a useful purpose.

Dear Lord,
Help us to pay attention to the one-way signs and to remember that traveling the wrong way on a one-way street will just get us to the wrong place quicker. Amen.

"...different rules for different drivers."

12
TRUCK ROUTE

"But he who respects a command is rewarded."
Proverbs 13:13

I'VE NEVER BEEN A truck driver; I mean a professional who drives a big semitrailer truck. But I have noticed the *Truck Route* signs that direct these drivers to different roads around towns and cities than the ones I usually take. I surmise that the purpose of this is to avoid congested and narrow areas or to keep heavy loads off certain roads or maybe even to expedite the truckers' journey on to their ultimate destinations. For whatever reason, this sign indicates that in various circumstances and for good reasons there are different rules for different drivers. The rules of life can also be like that. For example, my background, training, qualifications, and experience plus the load I carry can cause me to take a different route on my journey than others may take on theirs.

Dear Lord,
Thank you for truck drivers who accept the fact that at times they must take a different route for the benefit and safety of us all. Help me be like those who follow the rules. Amen.

"…many roads we should never travel."

13
DO NOT ENTER

"The highway of the upright avoids evil; he who guards his way guards his life."
Proverbs 16:17

SOME ROADS ARE REALLY confusing. For example, to the east of the city where I live, there is a congested maze of roadways popularly called "Spaghetti Junction." Two major interstate highways plus several other connecting roads come together at that point. Drivers are constantly entering and exiting from numerous directions. Situations like this and other similar ones call for an additional sign warning us against entering certain arteries where proceeding the wrong way would lead to disaster. Life is full of *Do Not Enter* signs; there are many roads we should never travel. In most dangerous situations, some type of warning sign or signal is there for us, if only we are alert and receptive to it. Interestingly, a companion to *Do Not Enter* is often a *Wrong Way* sign.

Dear Lord,
The dangers that abound on the highways of life are not always obvious to us. Please place **Do Not Enter** *signs at those junctures to keep us from going the wrong way. Amen.*

"...slow down and observe..."

14

SPEED BUMP

"An anxious heart weighs a man down.."
Proverbs 12:25

WE HAVE A LAKE house in the mountains that's about a three-hour drive from here. The contrast in the amount of traffic here and there is indicative of the different paces of the lifestyles in the city and in the country. We begin our trip passing a busy mall; this is followed by stints on interstate and on four-lane and two-lane highways. We even pass through a gorge that meanders around a small river. Immediately after we turn on to our road, a *Speed Bump* sign appears. It not only warns us but also reminds us that it's time to slow down and observe one of God's most magnificent masterpieces: a beautiful lake here among the Great Smoky Mountains. Our busy schedules ease, our pulse rates drop, and we breathe a bit slower as our spirits rise in anticipation of this time of rest and reflection.

Dear Lord,

Speed bumps are vivid reminders that we should not only slow down but also look around. We do not want to miss some of your greatest blessings. Please place more of them in our paths. Amen.

"...don't always make sense to us..."

15
NO U-TURN

*"There is a way that seems right to man,
but in the end it leads to death."*
Proverbs 16:25

WHEN WE ARE DRIVING, there are times when we need to turn around and go in the opposite direction. This occurred to me recently when I discovered that I was going the wrong way. I decided to turn around at the next intersection, but hanging there was a *No U-Turn* sign. I had to go a couple more miles before I could change course. I don't know exactly why that sign was at that particular intersection. Maybe there wasn't enough room to turn (I could have made it my little car) or there was too much traffic or an accident had occurred there. But I concluded that we need to follow the rules even though we don't always understand the reasons for them. To be honest, life's rules designed for our good don't always make sense to us, even when we are headed in the wrong direction.

Dear Lord,

If we need to turn our lives around, help us identify when and where so we can feel secure in that decision. May we trust your divine wisdom in your placement of No U-Turn *signs along the way. Amen.*

"...not viewed as a noble trait."

16
NO HORN BLOWING

*"A hot-tempered man stirs up dissention, but
a patient man calms a quarrel."*
Proverbs 15:18

IT'S MY BELIEF THAT a car horn has only a couple of purposes: first, to alert others in an attempt to avoid a collision or accident, and second, to let people know that you have arrived to pick them up. Maybe in a few other instances, there are also legitimate reasons. But, in general, "tooting your own horn" is not viewed as a noble trait. I have seen *No Horn Blowing* signs only in a few locations—in a hospital zone, near a funeral home, and on city streets and in private neighborhoods here and there. To reiterate, horn blowing for the right reasons has merit. So I believe that the sign should imply "no horn blowing in anger or for personal gratification." My image of a horn blower is a New York City cab driver. It is interesting to observe how something can be misused more often than appropriately used.

Dear Lord,

   Please remind me that I should blow my horn only for the right reasons, and help me not to toot it for the wrong ones. Amen.

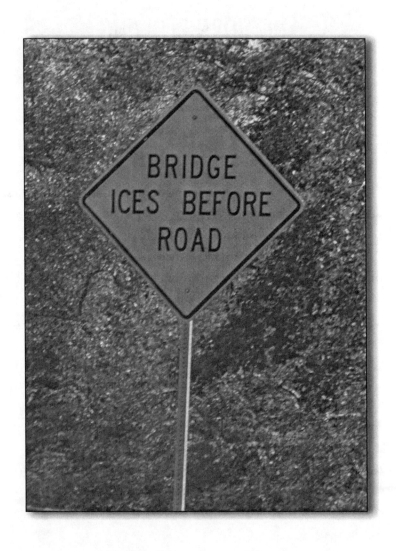

"Let's not discount seasonal messages…"

17
BRIDGE ICES BEFORE ROAD

*"Like snow in summer or rain in harvest,
honor is not fitting for a fool."*
Proverbs 26:1

IT'S THE MIDDLE OF July and ninety-five degrees as I'm driving down the highway. Up ahead I see a *Bridge Ices before Road* sign. What an out-of-place message! During the summer, the highway department should remove all such signs, but is that practical? There are probably hundreds or maybe even thousands of these around the state. What we must realize is that certain signs are seasonal, and they apply only at certain times or under extreme circumstances. In this case, the warning is for the wintertime, during ice storms or snowstorms. This fact does not make this particular sign less important; to the contrary, it may be the most critical one six months from now. Let's not discount seasonal messages along our paths. In this case, it may prevent skidding on a frozen bridge when winter comes.

Dear Lord,
We realize that we pass through various seasons of life on our journey home. Help us not only to see a sign but also to know when it applies. Amen.

"…keep us on the straight and narrow."

18
LOW AND SOFT SHOULDER

"A discerning man keeps wisdom in view, but a fool's eyes wander to the ends of the earth."
Proverbs 17:24

A PHYSICIAN FRIEND OF mine told a great story about two of his older patients. They were sisters in their late eighties, and the younger one could still drive. Returning from a short trip, the older sister noticed that the car was too close to the edge of the road, so she exclaimed, "Be careful, we are too close to the shoulder!" To which the younger one answered, "Oh, am I driving?" It's humorous, but I can remember times when my mind was wandering and I could have answered the same way. A *Low and Soft Shoulder* sign alongside the road is something we don't always observe, yet real danger can lurk there. Constant focus on the task at hand can keep us on the straight and narrow.

Dear Lord,
We can be distracted and our eyes can wander so easily in this high-speed world. Thank you for signs that remind us that even shoulders along the road we travel can be dangerous. Amen.

"...narrower than the road..."

19

NARROW BRIDGE AHEAD

"In the paths of the wicked lie thorns and snares, but he who guard his soul stays far from them."
Proverbs 22:5

OVER THE YEARS, MANY roads have been widened, probably to accommodate larger automobiles and trucks. This is relatively inexpensive; however, widening the bridges along the way is much more complicated and costly. Many roads, particularly local and rural ones, still have *Narrow Bridges* that cross rivers, creeks, railroad tracks, and other roads. Therefore, it has become necessary to alert drivers that the bridges may be narrower than the road or without a shoulder and an outside lane. Often there is little room for error there, and increased focus is required. At the same time, there can be distractions like a small, winding river below. Here again, we need constant concentration during our few seconds on the bridge.

Dear Lord,
As we cross the many narrow bridges on our way home, please help us not to be distracted so we may arrive safely at our ultimate destination. Amen.

"...a means to call for help."

20
CALL BOX

"Blessed is the man who listens to me."
Proverbs 8:33

WE CROSSED THE STATE line into Florida on I-75 and then headed east on a rather desolate area on I-10 to visit friends near St. Augustine. Along the way, we noticed under every mileage sign there was a *Call Box*. They were there for emergencies and could be activated by just turning a lever. A quick calculation reveals that a driver would never be more than half a mile from one of these at any time. Our first reaction was that this is old technology and no longer needed in this day of cell phones, iPhones and smartphones. But, we agreed, not everyone has one of these modern marvels. At about that time, my wife attempted to call one of our children, only to discover that we were in a dead zone, making our cell phones useless. We felt a degree of comfort knowing that, under any circumstances, we had a means to call for help. One of these call boxes was even at the rest area.

Dear Lord,
　　We are so thankful that we have a direct line always available to you. Help us never to forget that you are there twenty-four hours every day and that we need to call often, even just to talk. Amen.

"I smile every time I hear the click."

21
CLICK IT OR TICKET

"A wise son [and grandson] brings joy to his father [and grandfather]."
Proverbs 10:1

OUR STATE, LIKE OTHERS, has a mandatory seat-belt law. Until recent years, we had no such rules. Today, Georgia's roadways are full of *Click It or Ticket* signs, a catchy way to warn that you can be ticketed (and fined) for not wearing a seat belt. Because this was not part of my routine when the law was first passed, I more often than not found myself without my belt on. Then one day when three of my grandchildren were in the back seat, I heard a soft yet authoritative voice say, "Pappy, you need to put on your seat belt!" Today, I always click it, not because I might get a ticket, but because Nathan told me to. And I smile every time I hear the click.

Dear Lord,
Thank you for giving us wisdom through the voices and love of little cherubs and all the others who positively influence our actions. We feel snug and safe in your seat belts on our journey home. Amen.

"...grip the steering wheel securely..."

22
UNEVEN PAVEMENT

*"Now then, my sons, listen to me; do not turn
aside from what I say. Keep to a path."*
Proverbs 5:7

A PARKWAY NEAR MY home is in the process of being expanded from two to three lanes in both directions. This has been quite a project because it's one of the most traveled arteries in this section of the county. After almost a year of construction, the final coat of asphalt is now being laid one lane at a time. As a result, lanes are uneven until all are resurfaced, and *Uneven Pavement* signs are constantly being repositioned. Though it's best to stay in one lane, at times there is the need to cross over into another. I have discovered that it's really not hard to do if you grip the steering wheel securely and move over gradually. This makes me think about the fact that our individual life paths can also become uneven. It would certainly be helpful to have reminders of this so we can get a strong grip on the steering wheel that determines our direction.

Dear Lord,
As we move from lane to lane on life's highway, please warn us when the pavement is about to become uneven. Gosh, it seems like more often than not, it is uneven. And help us to learn to compensate. Amen.

"A mere glance at it speaks volumes…"

23
NO PARKING

"Do not... Do not... Do not... Do not...
Do not... Do not... Do not..."
Proverbs 23:3–20

IN MOST CASES, YOU can predict where a particular road sign will be. However, there is one sign that seems to show up in a multitude of places. It might be on a ramp exiting an interstate highway, around a busy intersection, at an entrance to commercial or public buildings, by a fire hydrant, and at many other sites. This is the familiar *No Parking* sign, and there are good reasons that parking is not permitted in such places. Parking a car there can be disruptive, intrusive, or even dangerous. This particular sign often contains no words, but the familiar large P with a line drawn through it is universally recognized. A mere glance at it speaks volumes and is loud and clear in its message to all of us: do not park here at any time. I have a special appreciation for this sign because it's neither ambiguous nor does its message leave any doubt. It says what it means and means what it says. I need that sometimes, because it's easy to become lax and even complacent in my habits behind the wheel.

Dear Lord,
You know when I need to hear, "Do not do that." Thanks for the signs that provide direct instructions and don't beat around the bush. And thanks for placing them in just the right places. Amen.

"We share responsibility for these other creatures…"

24
DEER CROSSING

"A loving doe, a graceful deer…"
Proverbs 5:19

ALONG THE HIGHWAYS AND roads, there are all sorts of crossing signs, but this particular one is unusual. There's a *Deer Crossing* sign on the main road I turn off of to get to my home. This is strange, because I live in a highly populated section of a metropolitan area of around five million people. Why in the world would a deer choose to live in a place like this and take a chance on crossing this busy road? It's simple; we live next to a three-thousand-acre national park. From time to time, deer, turkeys, foxes, raccoons, opossums, and other animals and fowl venture from their protected habitat into the hustle and bustle of city life. And in so doing, they tend to follow certain pathways that are marked by a sign such as this. It can be deadly when these beautiful animals find themselves standing or running in the path of a four-thousand-pound missile traveling at fifty-plus miles per hour. *Deer Crossing* as well as other similar signs call us to slow down and watch. We share responsibility for these other creatures that share this earth with us.

Dear Lord,
Help us to anticipate and avoid colliding with those who innocently find themselves in our paths. Someday, we ourselves may be in a similar position. Amen.

"...how quickly our journeys can be disrupted."

25

ROCK SLIDES

*"The prudent see danger and take refuge, but
the simple keep going and suffer for it."*
Proverbs 27:12

SEVERAL YEARS AGO, WHILE up at our vacation home in the mountains, we received word that a major rock slide had occurred north of us. Fortunately, there were no injuries, but the incident blocked a major interstate highway between two cities. The road was impassable for many months, which caused traffic to be diverted through various undesirable routes. Commerce, tourism, and community activities were adversely affected at both ends of the closed highway. Eventually, the debris was removed and the road repaired, but it left a lasting impression on all of us who live in, drive through, and visit those imposing mountains. Today, many *Rock Slide* signs give warning at strategic points along roads in that area, reminding us just how quickly our journeys can be disrupted.

Dear Lord,
We realized that from time to time things can come crashing down on us. Thank you for placing warning signs as we pass through steep canyons along the way, and please give us eyes and minds to recognize and react to potential danger. Amen.

"…it seems tranquil and even inviting…"

26
KEEP OFF THE MEDIAN

*"There is a way that seems right to man,
but in the end it leads to death."*
Proverbs 16:25

AS YOU DRIVE THROUGH the countryside on a four-lane highway, there is often a median in the middle. It is usually covered with green grass, wildflowers, or other landscape features. This attractive in-between space has never looked ominous to me; to the contrary, it seems tranquil and even inviting at times. However, one day this impression changed dramatically for me. While returning home from a trip, we rounded a curve and witnessed an automobile flipping over and over in the median. We and several others stopped to give aid and learned that a truck had forced the car onto the median. Evidently, the car hit a soft area in the median that spun it sideways, causing it to roll over at least five times. Police and emergency medical services arrived shortly. The injuries of the car's occupants appeared extensive to us, and though we tried, we never learned the outcome of this terrible accident. However, today we look at medians differently and take *Keep Off the Median* signs very seriously. Sometimes things that seem to be harmless can instead be treacherous.

Dear Lord,
　　In our travels we can easily be misled by things that appear attractive. Yet danger can lie just beneath the surface. Help us to heed the warnings and thus avoid the soft spots that can flip us over. Amen.

"...greatly hampers the ability to see..."

27
FOG AREA

"Let your eyes look straight ahead, fix your gaze directly before you."
Proverbs 4:25

MY EXPERIENCE WITH FOG has mainly been over the small lake in my back yard in the spring and fall. In this case, fog is like a ground-level cloud caused by cool or dry air meeting the warm water of the lake. However, fog also occurs on roadways. When the conditions are right, it's more prevalent in valleys and lowland areas, and it greatly hampers the ability to see the road clearly. But fortunately, based on history, certain places along the highways can be identified as fog areas. When confronting fog while driving, my tendency was to put on my bright lights, but I quickly learned that didn't help. Interestingly, using the lower beam was the better approach to ensure maximum visibility. I can recall several major accidents in our region caused by foggy conditions. *Fog Area* signs not only warn us of potential danger but also advise us to take appropriate preventive measures: slow down, use low beams, and keep your eyes on the road. At times along my life's journey, I have found myself in a fog.

Dear Lord,
   Sometimes we can lose sight of the road because of the foggy conditions in which we find ourselves. Please place **Fog Area** *signs in our paths and be the beam of light that guides us through these dangerous times of poor visibility. Amen.*

"...need to meet important standards..."

28
WEIGH STATION

"The Lord abhors dishonest scales, but accurate weights are his delight."
Proverbs 11:1

I'M SURE YOU HAVE noticed more than once a line of trucks slowing down in the right lane of a major highway. Then you see the *Weigh Station* sign. My usual reaction is that I'm glad I'm not driving a big truck. I have a hard enough time maneuvering my full-size SUV. Obviously, we know that each truck's weight is to be checked on a scale, but I didn't realize that these stations do much more to ensure safety than enforce laws and regulations. For example, tire load, road width, bridge height, and other conditions are all taken into consideration during the inspections. While on our life journeys, we, like those big trucks, need to meet important standards that will ensure a safe arrival home. And periodic inspections can be helpful in this regard. There may even be times when we attempt to carry a load that is too heavy or our tires are almost flat.

Dear Lord,
Please measure the weight, depth, and height of our values, our convictions, our commitment, and our love. And guide us in our efforts to pass inspection so we can successfully complete our journey. Amen.

"... too fast to maintain control..."

29
RUNAWAY TRUCK RAMP

*"But whoever listens to me will live in safety
and be at ease, without fear of harm."*
Proverbs 1:33

LET'S TALK ABOUT TRUCKS one more time. I have a large SUV that is difficult to maneuver; I can only imagine how challenging driving a large semitrailer truck might be. When we are up in the Great Smokies, I notice how difficult it is for these massive vehicles to climb the steeps, but on the other hand how fast they can travel when descending the mountains. I'm told that at times these trucks must remain in a lower gear, and certainly good brakes are imperative when coming down the mountains. I'm sure it doesn't happen often, but occasionally something can go wrong, and a truck's speed becomes too fast to maintain control. At strategic places, you will notice a *Runaway Truck Ramp* sign that indicates that an escape route is just ahead. Recently, I noticed deep ruts in a sand-filled ramp that evidently were the result of a prudent truck driver using it. This caused me to think about the times life seems to be racing out of control down a winding mountain, and without an escape route, a disaster most certainly lies ahead.

Dear Lord,

In the ups and downs of life, we sometime travel at an excessive speed, particularly when we are coming down from the top of a mountain. We can't maintain control under these conditions, so please place escape ramps in the most dangerous areas. Amen.

"...we experience zigs and zags..."

30
WINDING ROAD

*"Get wisdom, get understanding; do not forget
my words or swerve from them."*
Proverbs 4:5

ROADS THAT WIND AROUND like snakes can be found anywhere, but they are more prevalent in mountainous areas. On one occasion, I observed a severely winding road through the middle of a small, rural community in a flat region. I later learned that it was planned that way to cross over railroad tracks not once but several times. This provided more access to freight cars transporting goods. I'm very conscious of such roads because they can be a major cause of motion sickness. Even beyond that, when a car is going around winding roads, there is added danger and an increased need to be focused and alert. At times, we experience zigs and zags in our personal lives that can be upsetting and even dangerous. Therefore, *Winding Road* signs can help us anticipate them.

Dear Lord,
When drastic curves in our roads appear, warn us so we can decelerate, avoid swerving, and hold it on the road. And please prescribe some spiritual Dramamine for us. Amen.

"…on their way to help someone."

31
FIRE STATION

*"Have no fear of sudden disaster... for the
Lord will be your confidence."*
Proverbs 3:25–26

IF YOU ARE LIKE me, you drive past certain road signs so often you forget not only that they are there but also the message they convey. The other day I was on one of my routine routes and noticed a blinking light above the roadway ahead. Traffic had come to a standstill, and then I realized why. A fire truck with lights on and siren blasting came whisking out, undoubtedly to respond to a call. It could have been a fire, an auto accident, or some other type of emergency. For whatever reason, they were on their way to help someone. I was several cars back in the line of those stopped, but as traffic began to move, I saw it—the *Fire Station* sign. Though I was delayed a few minutes from reaching my destination, I felt pride that my tax dollars pay for services like that. And I was also reminded that we have brave men and women who are willing to risk their lives to assist others.

Dear Lord,
Help me not to become complacent and miss the significance of signs. And thank you for calling good folks to give of themselves in such meaningful ways. Amen.

"…we all have handicaps of some sort."

32
HANDICAP PARKING

"The name of the Lord is a strong tower."
Proverbs 18:10

YOU WILL FIND THIS sign on some streets but mainly in parking lots in front of business establishments. Actually, laws prescribe the number of these, depending on the type and size of a business. I'm most familiar with the *Handicap Parking* sign when we visit my mother-in-law, who has a parking permit to use such spaces. She is ninety-four, lives alone, and is still active as an artist. Her paintings go to support various charitable causes. She is very outspoken, fearlessly independent, and one of the strongest yet most caring individuals I've ever known. She qualifies for these parking places because she uses a walker. *Handicapped* is not a term I would use to describe her. But after giving this some thought, I guess we all have handicaps of some sort. After a bout with cancer, our grandson has a weakness on one side, and among my many limitations are hearing loss and a high golf handicap. There are many more examples; such is the nature of us humans.

Dear Lord,
We realize that we, like all your children, are handicapped in one way or another. Help us to remember that though we are weak, you are strong. Amen.

"…looking for alternative means of transportation."

33
SHARE THE ROAD

"A man's wisdom gives him patience."
Proverbs 19:11

WITH THE COST OF gas today, some folks are looking for alternative means of transportation. In this regard, I've noticed more people riding bicycles, and not just for recreation. A doctor friend of mine bikes almost ten miles to work every day. He's not only saving gas and reducing pollution, but also is in fabulous physical shape. My frame of reference on this subject was a visit to the People's Republic of China in the 1980s, where bicycles on the roads outnumbered automobiles probably a thousand to one. This approach to travel has prompted some communities to widen streets to add a narrow lane on the outside designated for bikes. These and other stretches of road often have a sign that prompts drivers to *Share the Road*. When scurrying from place to place, we can get impatient with bikers on the road. But let's remember the positive effect on the environment and how much better off we would be if we followed their example. So, as I carefully pass them, I wave as a statement of approval and encouragement.

Dear Lord,
Make us conscious of your earth's environment and of the condition of our own bodies. Help us to embrace habits that improve both. Amen.

"…just have to pay a little extra…"

34
TOLL ROAD

"One man gives freely, yet gains even more."
Proverbs 11:24

A ROADWAY ON WHICH you must pay a fee to drive is called a toll road. Usually this charge is necessary to cover either the original cost of its construction or continuous maintenance. Some bridges and tunnels have tolls for similar reasons. The toll is usually collected at a booth or through some type of prepaid system. I resented having to pay this; after all, I already paid taxes to provide adequate highways and streets. With this negative attitude, I was struggling for a valid life message that a *Toll Road* sign delivers. When I raised this concern with one of my brothers-in-law, without hesitation he commented, "There are times that you just have to pay a little extra to get to where you need to be on time." He wasn't looking on the spiritual side, but I believe that Earl hit the nail on the head. That faster route home would probably not exist without a toll being charged.

Dear Lord,
   Help us to realize that there are times when we need to pay extra and give more on life's journey in order to arrive home on time. Help me not to resent the toll. Amen.

"...something special about things that are old..."

35
HISTORICAL DISTRICT

"Gray hair is a crown of splendor; it is attained by a righteous life."
Proverbs 16:31

I IMAGINE NEARLY ALL cities and towns have historical districts. However, ours has one of the most interesting and intriguing that I have ever seen; history abounds here. Because a major Civil War battle occurred in our very neighborhood, it is not unusual to find artifacts in our own backyard. Among the most fascinating aspects of the past are the beautifully restored homes that date back before the War Between the States. *Historical District* signs guide us to neighborhoods where architectural marvels are prevalent. I've never considered myself a history buff, but I do have a genuine interest in the significant happenings and experiences of those who came before us. When we have guests, we enjoy driving them through this district, and they are always amazed. There is something special about things that are old yet have endured. Understanding and appreciating the past adds to the quality of the present and the richness of the future.

Dear Lord,
  Help us to see and understand what has gone before us so we can learn not to repeat the wrongs of the past but instead to emulate those things that were right. Let history be our guide. Amen.

"…in full view from above."

36
PHOTO ENFORCED

*"For a man's ways are in full view of the Lord,
and he examines all his paths."*
Proverbs 5:21

I DON'T KNOW IF this is going on in your community, but in ours there is a new law-enforcement technique that's resulting in many tickets and fines. At certain busy intersections, a camera records the license plates of cars that speed through the yellow light instead of beginning to stop for the red one that follows. Fortunately, this has not happen to me, but several of my friends have received citations in the mail that included this indisputable evidence that the law was violated. Interestingly, many of these intersections are marked with *Photo Enforced* signs as you approach them. Some are objecting to this new intervention, claiming a violation of privacy, but I haven't heard anyone deny that the violations occurred. In our community, if you pay the fine immediately, the first infraction is not permanently placed on your driving record. All this new technology, like cameras looking down on us, makes our driving habits much more transparent. Interestingly, our spiritual ones have always been in full view from above.

Dear Lord,
   Help us to remember that you are not only all seeing but also all knowing. And constantly remind us that all the rules you have established are for our own good. Amen.

"…nothing more precious to us than our children."

37
SCHOOL

"Children's children are a crown to the aged."
Proverbs 17:6

WHEN APPROACHING A SCHOOL zone, you begin to see a multitude of signs calling this to your attention. School crossings, school bus stops, a myriad of symbols, and always a decreased speed limit sign greet you. Why so many? I believe it's because there is probably nothing more precious to us than our children. Reading about an accident, major injury, illness, or any disaster involving kids horrifies and grips us like nothing else. When our grandson was diagnosed with neuroblastoma, a form of pediatric cancer, despair greater that anything we could imagine consumed us. There is probably no sign that I honor more than a *School* sign. When passing the school grounds and observing the kids on the playground, I smile. Then I remember how blessed we are to have Nathan, our third-grade grandson, out there playing with the others—now six years in remission.

Dear Lord,

Thank you for schools and students and particularly for those special folks that teach them. Help us to remember not only to slow down as we pass a school but also to cherish our children just like you do. Amen.

"Something special and noble is happening…"

38
ADOPT A HIGHWAY

"He who seeks good finds goodwill."
Proverbs 11:27

ADOPTION IS A WONDERFUL act of love and commitment, but it also brings responsibility. Years ago, my sister and her husband adopted three children, and recently my niece and husband adopted a little boy. But adopting a road—what's that all about? In my search, I began to notice signs like A*dopt a Highway … a Road … a Street … a Mile.* The adopting parents in these cases are usually organizations, civic clubs, churches, and even families. However, I realized that this program was more than just a sign. I observed folks picking up trash and debris, planting bushes and seasonal flowers, and beautifying the roadsides in other ways. I realized that transportation departments are responsible for the landscaping and maintenance of our road systems, but, by involving volunteers, a personal touch has been added that brings joy to passing travelers. Something special and noble is happening when we accept the responsibility of improving the paths for others. And, as a result, all are blessed.

Dear Lord,
Please constantly remind us to adopt habits and practices that will improve and enhance the journey of our fellow travelers along life's way. Then we can claim with assurance that our life has not been in vain. Amen.

"…to create a smoother and safer traffic flow…"

39
ROUNDABOUT

"A man who strays from the path of understanding comes to rest in the company of the dead."
Proverbs 21:16

I'VE ONLY BEEN EXPOSED to roundabouts in recent years, and I'm finally getting comfortable navigating the few in our area. A roundabout is a circular intersection that flows in one direction around a central island. Its purpose is to create a smoother and safer traffic flow at certain dangerous intersections. It's sort of a "traffic circle" where those entering must yield to vehicles already in the circle. It is also important to position yourself to exit onto the desired intersecting street. If you have never used a roundabout during your travels, this may be confusing. However, once you have maneuvered through one, you soon realize how helpful it can be to speed you safely on your way. The *Roundabout* road sign is intriguing to me, with its arrows pointing circularly in one direction. As we travel, it's good to be reminded how important it is that, during times of heavy traffic at dangerous intersections, all of us drive in the same direction.

Dear Lord,
As we approach a roundabout sign in our travels, remind us that we live in a world fraught with danger that can be minimized when we follow your instructions. Help us to proceed in the same direction with others who are on the path toward home. Amen.

"...habits of just making a mess..."

40
NO THROWING TRASH

*"The way of the sluggard is blocked with thorns,
but the path of the upright is a highway."*
Proverbs 15:19

ONLY A FEW PUNITIVE road signs post the penalty that can result from breaking the law. In our state, the *No Throwing Trash on the Highway* sign does just that. I don't know why some indicate potential fines and others don't, but let me speculate. In the case of littering, some folks have developed habits of just making a mess and leaving it for someone else to clean up. A drink can, snack sack, napkin, or cigarette butt thrown out the window of an automobile doesn't seem like a lot. But, if allowed, before long a collage of debris would deface the beautiful landscapes that border our roads and highways. I once thought a sign like *Treat Our Road Like It Is Your Home* would have emotional appeal but later realized that many don't clean up their act at home either. Certainly nobody's perfect, but I hope on my journey's path I can claim that littering was neither one of my physical nor one of my spiritual habits. Besides, I can't afford a $1,200 fine.

Dear Lord,
We get lax with our habits and before long realize what a mess we have made. Help us practice cleanliness as next to godliness as we travel the highways toward home. Amen.

"...the light at the end of it."

41
TUNNEL

*"The path of the righteous is like the first gleam of dawn,
shining ever brighter till the full light of day."*
Proverbs 4:18

WE HAVE A FEW tunnels in our mountains. Sometime there is no other way to reach the other side. I also remember driving under a body of water in a similar confined stretch. I have mixed feelings when I drive through a tunnel. I tend to tense up a bit because of the narrow lanes, which require extra concentration; I imagine this is where the term "tunnel vision" originated. You keep your headlights on while viewing only concrete or rock on both sides and above. Though a tunnel is void of the beauty found in open spaces, it is amazing in its own way. So when I see a *Tunnel* sign, I get excited because I realize that I'm about to experience something very different from my normal drive home. And I'll arrive there much earlier because the tunnel eliminates the need to take a much longer route. However, I must confess that the best part of a tunnel is the light at the end of it.

Dear Lord,

Thank you for tunnels that provide routes home when there are barriers, such as mountains and rivers, that impede our journey. But, most of all, we are grateful for the illumination we experience as we return to the Light of the World. Amen.

"...the saddest ones on the road..."

42
THEY KILL (DUI) DON'T DO IT

*"Wine is a mocker and beer a brawler; whoever
is led astray by them is not wise."
Proverbs 20:1*

YEARS AGO IN OUR local newspaper, names and photographs (mug shots) were published of those convicted of drunk driving, which was both humiliating and embarrassing. More highway accidents and fatalities result from someone driving under the influence than from any other cause. Driving Under the Influence, the term used today, includes not only alcohol but also drugs that impair driving ability. *They Kill (DUI) Don't Do It* signs are perhaps the saddest ones on the road to me. The fact that they are necessary is a reminder of human frailty, bad judgment, and a lack of responsibility. I'm not certain that there is such a thing as spiritual DUI, but I believe that there are self-administered potions that tend to numb and distort our spiritual senses. Self-centeredness, greed, jealousy, and hatred are just a few culprits, and all result in negative happenings. Unfortunately, there is a need for signs that remind us to refrain from placing ourselves under the influence of things that will bring harm.

Dear Lord,
Please keep us close to you so we do not fall under the influence of things that blur both our physical and our spiritual vision. Help us to remain sober and responsible throughout our journey. Amen.

"…became my spiritual home…"

43
CHURCH

"The name of the Lord is a strong tower; the righteous run to it and are safe."
Proverbs 18:10

IT'S A BIT UNUSUAL to see this sign on a public road anymore. The presence of a *Church* sign seems to offend certain folks, so the usual reaction is to remove it. These days some can find fault with almost anything. After observing this sign the other day, I saw the building; it was over one hundred years old and still open and active. The parking lot was small, so the membership probably wasn't very large, but I would bet it had many long-term parishioners. As I drove by, I imagined the effects this little church has had on people's lives and the contributions it has made in this small community and beyond for so many years. Then I began to feel a deep sense of pride because this great institution has played such a significant role in my life. You see, I'm a PK (preacher's kid), so from the beginning I considered the church to be my father's workplace, but then it also became my spiritual home, the Body of Christ.

Dear Lord,
Thank you for the church, the great institution you have charged with the responsibility to spread your word of faith, hope, and love. Help us to find our place in the Body of Christ so we can help others find their way home. Amen.

"Lights from others help guide us…"

44
LIGHTS ON WHEN RAINING

"The light of the righteous shines brightly."
Proverbs 13:9

WE WERE RETURNING HOME from a visit with friends when we found ourselves driving into a heavy rainstorm. It was midafternoon, and only a few miles earlier the sun had been shining brightly. During the next hour or so, we found ourselves alternately passing from clear to stormy stretches. On one occasion, the rain and sunshine actually appeared simultaneously (an old wives tale was that this meant the devil was beating his wife). Then I saw the sign *Lights on When Raining.* So, following instructions, I turned my headlights on. But this didn't improve my ability to see the road very much. Then I realized that the purpose of this sign's message was to help me see the other cars in front and in back of me. And the reason for having mine on was so they could better see me. Lights from others help guide us through many of life's storms. In this case, the sign also reminded me to do for others things that I would have them to for me: turn on my lights.

Dear Lord,

Sometimes we don't realize that we need to let our lights shine for the benefit of others. Help us to be mindful of your rules of reciprocity that instruct us to help one another throughout our journeys. Amen.

"...they serve a vital purpose."

45

TERRAPIN XING

"A righteous man cares for the needs of his animal."
Proverbs 12:10

ONE OF THE EARLIER road signs in this book cited animal crossings, but this particular one needs to be given special attention. I spied it as we drove onto the causeway through the Marshes of Glynn to St. Simons Island, Georgia. Terrapins, or turtles as we call them in the Deep South, are slow-moving reptiles that live around lakes and swamps. The marshes are the natural habitat of the diamondback terrapin. Some of our human activities, such as building a highway through the marsh, have disrupted its migration, feeding, and reproduction patterns. A turtle is pretty helpless when crossing a busy four-lane causeway during the nesting season (May–July). I honestly don't know all the attributes of turtles, but I have no doubt that they serve a vital purpose. Therefore, I'm proud that some conservationists have raised the awareness of the plight of this special little creature. The *Terrapin Xing* sign not only raised my consciousness level and slowed me down, but also reminded me that the terrapin beat the hare to the finish line.

Dear Lord,
We aren't reminded often enough that you placed us on the earth to be stewards of your creation. Help us to be constantly aware of the fact that you created and blessed all the animals, including the lowly turtle. Amen.

"…there are also times to leave…"

46
EVACUATION ROUTE

"When calamity overtakes you like a storm, when disaster sweeps over you like a whirlwind…"
Proverbs 1:27

ON TWO OCCASIONS, I lived in a coastal city that was subject to hurricanes. When I was growing up, weather forecasting was neither as sophisticated nor accurate as today. So hurricane season was foremost on our minds. However, even though these storms are just as powerful and destructive as ever, lives are now being saved that once would have been lost. This is primarily because meteorological advances have resulted in better preparation for the onslaught of horrendous weather. Recently, on an interstate highway, I noticed *Hurricane Evacuation Route* signs. There were also mechanical arms at the foot of each ramp ready to be raised or lowered to control traffic in the face of an approaching hurricane. Certainly there are occasions when we are to stand firm, but there are also times to evacuate during the storms of life. Sadly, some ignore the warnings and suffer the consequences.

Dear Lord,
We often find ourselves in the midst of spiritual weather disturbances. The rains are heavy and the winds are strong. Please guide us by marking the evacuation route from the storms of evil. Amen.

"…these beautiful landscape scenes…"

47
SCENIC VIEW

*"The Lord possessed me at the beginning of his work…
when there were no oceans… before the mountains
were settled in place… I was given birth."
Proverbs 8:22–25*

AS YOU DRIVE THROUGH some of the most picturesque parts of the country, you are invited from time to time to pull off on a short parallel road and absorb the beauty there. This happened to us in the North Carolina mountains this fall as we accepted an invitation to stop to view the magnificent Technicolor coat that the mountains wore. On another occasion, I experienced the wonder and awe of gazing down on the Oregon seashore. A *Scenic View* sign is an enticement to go into an art gallery like no other. The talents of the One who created these beautiful landscape scenes dwarf the combined talents of Rembrandt, Van Gogh, Michelangelo, Picasso, and all the great artists. The cost of the ticket to this wonderful exhibit is free, and I know the Artist personally. And, just think, I'm also part of His creation and you are, too.

Dear Lord,

You can do anything. We are so thankful that you allow us the privilege of observing and experiencing the incomparable beauty of your handiwork. And we really appreciate the complimentary tickets for front-row seats. Amen.

"...the anticipation that arises as you get closer..."

48
DESTINATION AND DISTANCE

"Listen, my son, and be wise, and keep your heart on the right path."
Proverbs 23:19

AS A YOUNG BOY on trips with family, I would continuously ask my dad, "How much longer before we get there?" My own children and now my grandchildren have asked the same question. We're all anxious to get there, particularly when our destination is home after some time away. There is one sign that helps with this; I call it the *Destination and Distance* road sign. It names upcoming towns and gives the mileage to each of them. The sign doesn't actually answer the question "How much longer?" but an experienced driver can calculate it by converting distance to time. To me, the more interesting aspect of these signs is the anticipation they cause as you get closer and closer to home. When I learned to make the approximate time-of-arrival calculation, I became much more conscious of this helpful road sign. As I mentioned earlier, I like to go places, but I love to come home. I know the name of my ultimate home and how many miles already traveled; so there is no doubt I'm getting closer every day.

Dear Lord,
Thank you for the many ways you encourage us and particularly for the signs you place in our paths to remind us we are getting closer to home. Amen.

"…*just a few minutes from home.*"

49
CITY LIMIT

"She takes her stand; beside the gates leading into the city…"
Proverbs 8:2–3

BECAUSE WE MOVED AROUND so often when I was growing up, I never considered one particular place my hometown. However, I have now given that title to the city in which we have lived for the past forty-three years. When I pass the Marietta *City Limit* sign, the message is loud and clear: we're just a few minutes from home. It's interesting how the tension and discomfort from a long drive begin to subside and a feeling of peace and comfort take their place. On this last leg of our destination, it is as if we are in an airplane making its decent and final approach for landing. I look out the window, spotting certain land marks, and think, *Home at last.* At times when I'm focused on important things, I speculate that the final approach to our ultimate home may be something like this. Instead of a traumatic experience, it will be more like crossing the city limit line into that city with streets of gold. By the way, my city limit sign says, "Welcome."

Dear Lord,
From your teachings, we can visualize our ultimate hometown as being one of beauty and wonder. Thanks for that special city limit sign that designated its entry—the cross. Amen.

"…don't consider it a dead end."

50
NO OUTLET

"Wisdom is found in those who take advice."
Proverbs 13:10

AT THE ENTRY INTO my neighborhood, next to the street sign is a *No Outlet* sign. Posted on a similar street is a *Dead End* sign. Our house is the last one on the street, and I like *No Outlet* better, because I don't consider it a dead end. To the contrary, my home is a new beginning. Every time I arrive home, I have a genuine feeling of peace, joy, and love. Of course, the purpose of the *No Outlet* sign is to tell those who enter that it is not a through street. And I'm okay with that, because when I turn onto Battlefield Road, I know I'm almost home.

Dear Lord,

Please help us to know where we are going in this life so we don't find ourselves at a dead end. And in this turbulent world, thank you for providing us a haven of peace, joy, and love called home. Amen.

"...reaping the rewards of first being parents."

51
SLOW GRANDPARENTS AT PLAY

"A good man leaves an inheritance for his children's children."
Proverbs 13:22

I HAD TO INCLUDE this one, though I must confess it was not placed on the road by the Department of Transportation. We bought it at a general store in the mountains, and it hangs on a post just as you enter our property. As folks come to visit, they chuckle and ask, "Does it mean that we need to drive slowly, or do you grandparents just play slowly?" And to both questions, we always answer, "Yes!" There are three key words in this sign. The first is *slow;* we need to slow down so we can smell the roses and enjoy life. The second is *grandparents,* who are some of the most blessed folks on earth because they reap the rewards of first being parents. And finally, *play* is an attribute that should be enjoyed irrespective of age. *Slow Grandparents at Play* is a fun little road sign, but it carries a most significant and powerful message.

Dear Lord,
   Thank you for the privilege we have of being grandparents. We realize that reaching this milestone means that we are a little closer to reaching home. When we arrive, please be patient with us as we tell you all about our grandchildren. Amen.

"Professionally We Serve, Personally We Care."

52
HOSPITAL

"Let love and faithfulness never leave you."
Proverbs 3:3

I'VE SAVED *HOSPITAL*, MY favorite, for the last road sign. This one is extra special to me because I spent my entire forty-year professional career working in hospitals. For all those many years, a hospital was my "work home." When I first started, my title was hospital administrator, and when I retired I was called a chief executive officer. My ego was fed by that CEO designation, but to be honest I felt more comfortable just being identified as a hospital administrator. *Administrator* is a derivative of the word *minister*, which means "to serve." My hospital system's credo for most of my tenure was "Professionally We Serve, Personally We Care." In times of need, a road sign that directs you to a hospital is invaluable. Loving folks who provide professional service and personal care faithfully await you there.

Dear Lord,
Thank you for hospitals and particularly for the doctors, nurses, technologists, service workers, and all those who serve and care for others. I truly believe that there is no greater calling than to serve and care for the sick. Amen.

"...a haven where love, joy, and peace reside."

HOME

"By wisdom a house is built, and through understanding it is established; through knowledge its rooms are filled with rare and beautiful treasures."
Proverbs 24:3–4

OUR HOUSE IS THE last one on Battlefield Road. Beyond our picket-fence entrance is a circular drive that leads right up to the front of the house. Family and friends always enter the side door, which leads directly into the kitchen. Inside, one of the first things you notice is a framed poem that was cross-stitched by my grandmother many years ago. It states, "Life's riches other rooms adorn, but in a kitchen, home is born." This is just the beginning; as you explore every room in the house, you realize you are no longer in a house just constructed with bricks and mortar. It comes alive with family and friends who share and experience together all aspects of life. But, most importantly, it becomes that haven where love, joy, and peace reside. This is where my journey ends. This is *Home!*

Dear Lord,

Thank you for giving me such a wonderful earthly home. I honestly believe this is just a foretaste of the ultimate home you have prepared for us. Most of all, thank you for not only placing those special road signs along our route, but also for traveling this journey with us. Amen.

BONUS: A FEW OTHER MESSAGES

My fixation with road signs has caused me to notice many messages during my travels. Some of these are serious and others are humorous, but irrespective of the tone, each has made me think. Here are just a few that caught my eye.

Billboards

Where extras are not extra (Drury Inn)
Clean "potties" and showers (a truck stop)
Made from scratch all day (Cracker Barrel)
Your best customer just drove by (sign rental)
"Well, you did ask for a sign."—God
Not vaccinated? No kisses. (a health care company)
Be up for being up for everything
EAT MOR CHIKIN (Chick-Fil-A)
Remember ... only you can prevent forest fires! (Smokey the Bear)
"Do you have any idea where you are going?"—God

Church Signs

God answers knee mail
Despite the rain, the Son will shine
"I want custody seven days a week, not just on Sundays"—God
Choose the Bread of Life or you are toast
Fight truth decay, study the Bible daily
Ask about our pray-as-you-go plan

Instead of telling God how big your problem is, tell your problem how big your God is.
Basic *Instructions* **Before** *Leaving* **Earth**—*Bible*
God Doesn't Call the Qualified. He Qualifies the Called
Free Trip to Heaven, Details Inside

T-shirts

Thy rod and thy reel they comfort me
I'm so far behind I thought I was first
Gobble Jog (Thanksgiving Road Race)
If you keep your mouth shut, you won't get caught (fisherman)
Remember, as far as anyone knows, we are a nice normal family
Change is good. You go first. (Dilbert)
Whatever It is, I Didn't Do It
It is what it is!
My job is so secret, I don't even know what I'm doing
PRAYER—The world's greatest wireless connection

Vehicle Signs (on cars and trucks)

More than a lake, an experience! (Lake Junaluska, North Carolina)
As long as there are tests, there will be prayer in schools (a bumper sticker)
OVERSIZE LOAD
We put our nose in other peoples' business (a plumbing company)
Don't Believe in Miracles, Rely on Them (a bumper sticker)
Holy Smoke (a barbecue)
Don't Wait for the Hearse to Take You to Church (a car plate)
The best things in life are not things (a bumper sticker)
No job is too big … or too small! (a painting contractor)
WIDE TURN Saf-T-1st

Other

WARNING
This Property is protected by an Armed American Veteran.
Absolutely nothing here worth dying for.
(alarm system sign)

REFLECTIONS AND CONCLUSIONS

The preparation of this work has been not only fascinating but also a real adventure for me. Picture a seventy-four-year-old fellow with his wife, stopping alongside interstates, four-lane and two-lane highways, and country roads, on neighborhood streets and alleys, and even on a few private drives to photograph road signs. That was us for almost a year. Many times I pulled the car to the roadside for a quick stop, and Snookie held her camera out the window to capture a coveted sign.

I learned quickly that this book was not one I could just sit down and write; each road sign and its message had to be explored individually. At the same time, I was pondering the book of Proverbs in more depth than ever before to identify correlations that might exist between the messages of particular verses and those of specific road signs. At first, I attempted to find a verse from Proverbs that fit a particular sign; however, soon this process began to reverse itself. I found myself discovering signs that carried the message of these verses, which were becoming more and more familiar to me as I repeatedly read and absorbed the content of this wonderful book.

While doing this, I also started to observe my surroundings in more detail. For example, in addition to road signs, I began noticing all sorts of other things that convey lessons. I paid more attention to billboards, bumper stickers, decals, license plates, marquees, bulletin boards, T-shirt inscriptions, and many other sources that attempted to communicate with me. Not in every instance but amazingly in many, I sensed a truth that was being expressed. So I have become infatuated with all types of message boards that teach *lessons*, define *principles*, and express *truths* that can be applied in our lives.

This venture has produced some interesting and positive side effects. For example, those of us who are classified as seniors are advised to exercise not only our bodies but also our minds to maintain good overall health. This project has been somewhat like a mental gymnastics class, but more than that, it has been a true spiritual experience. It has forced me to think out of my "usual routine" box.

In developing this manuscript, I typically identified and wrote one road sign message per day and then spent another day refining it. While this was going on, I was reading my Bible and we were on our constant hunt for the road signs. All this tended to keep me out of the troubles that many old folks like me experience: an idle mind, a body without motion, and spiritual apathy. I feel renewed and blessed because God put this simple thought in my mind: *road signs are our friends.* And remember, true friends always have our best interests at heart.

Hopefully, my brief explanation of this experience hasn't given you the impression that I have become more intellectually brilliant, philosophically enlightened, or theologically grounded. To the contrary, though I've chalked up many miles, I've concluded that in the broad scheme of things, I know very little. But, hopefully, in this exercise of observing the road signs along our paths toward home, both you and I have gained a little more wisdom and truth.

At this stage, I'm beginning to view things encountered in daily life differently than before. Having lived so long and experienced so much, the question that I tend to ask myself now is, "What difference does this really make?" In regard to this literary work, if it is just another book that will go on your shelf or in your e-book file, the effort falls far short of its purpose. If it has been just an interesting and entertaining mental exercise, I feel like I missed the mark. Even if it does make you more aware of signs and lessons, that is not enough. It is my hope that something as simple as road signs can constantly remind us what is important and help us remember our true purpose of life. And, as we journey toward our permanent and eternal homes, we will be drawn closer to each other and the God who made us. I pray that this little book will *really make a difference*! You will be the judge.

With that, I'll close with a final message from the amazing book of Proverbs:

> *"Trust in the Lord with all your heart and lean not on your own understanding; in all your ways acknowledge him, and he will make your paths straight"*
> *Proverbs 3:5-6*

EPILOGUE: PHOTOGRAPHY EXPERIENCES

While I have never aspired to be a professional photographer, my job as wife, mother, and grandmother has definitely positioned me to record family events of all kinds. Until the cell phone came on the scene, I always seemed to be the only one carrying a camera, with all the others expecting to get copies of whatever I recorded on film. So I guess it was the normal progression of things that led to my first official photography gig. For this book, Bernie needed pictures, and I had the camera.

In fact, I now have a digital camera that is small enough to fit in my purse, so it's almost always with me. Bernie, however, is known for his last-minute checklist. He always asks, "Do you have the directions? Do you have the tickets?" and so on. Thus, during this adventure, we never left the house without the question, "Do you have your camera?" Hearing that constant inquiry required much patience on my part, as my answer was always yes.

Even trips to the grocery store had potential for this project; we never knew when the "right" road sign would appear. Bernie's instructions went something like this: "Make sure you take the picture vertically. Don't get too close; it needs to have some scenery. Don't get too far away; can't read the words as well." My reward from him was, "Ah, that's just the right shot."

When I first tried my hand at getting it "just right," I discovered a line going down the center of each photo. It was a puzzle to me until something struck me: the seldom-noticed radio antenna on the front of our car was the culprit. It got in my way when I leaned out the window to snap a picture. Once I had solved that problem, the adventure began! It was like a treasure hunt as we traveled interstates, four-lane and two-lane highways, causeways, parkways, city streets, and country roads.

Some pictures were harder to get than others. How do you photograph a *Keep Off the Median* sign that tells you plainly to keep off the median? You get the camera ready and then quickly pull over on a desolate section when you don't see anyone coming for miles. Or you seek a weigh station that is closed for some reason and get a picture of the sign quickly, hoping no state patrol cars or huge trucks show up.

Another challenge was the *No U-turn* sign positioned on the driver's side. I had to let Bernie lean out for that one. Then there was the one posted above the tunnel, just around a curve. I had to be super trigger happy before traffic caught up with us. My favorite was on the roadside just before driving over the causeway on St. Simons Island. *Terrapin Xing*, the cutest of all the signs, was my target, but it required pulling into a park and climbing over a low fence and through some bushes to avoid the steady traffic on that stretch. I have to say that it was worth the effort.

We were on our way home from a funeral when we discovered the perfect *Winding Road* sign. My feet were hurting, so I was barefoot in the car. I couldn't imagine putting back on my shoes and walking a block, even for that great sign. So I hopped out without shoes and headed toward my goal. As I passed the corner of a church, a security guy walked out and gave me a long look before returning to his post. I guess he decided that a crazy lady in Sunday clothes with no shoes and only a camera in hand held no threat for the property in his care.

Despite our best efforts, there were some signs that we just couldn't find or photograph. In these few cases, a search of the Internet was just as adventurous. Our requests for assistance were rejected by some, but in other cases, we found willing and enthusiastic photographers who gladly gave permission for their photos to be a part of this project. And we are indeed grateful to them.

I seriously doubt I will be returning to school for a degree in photography, but it was a real joy to be able to share in the preparation of this fascinating book with my husband. I guess I will forever have a keen awareness of the signs that dot our landscape wherever we go.

Snookie Brown, wife and chief photographer

STUDY GUIDE

"What Difference Does This Really Make?"

I had not planned to include a study guide in this book, but a note from a dear friend prompted me to include one. Lucy Adams, an author and the cofounder of the Western North Carolina Christian Writers Fellowship, wrote, "My goodness, Bernie, this is amazing. Never thought of this… but it is simple and profound. We can see road signs differently after reading your devotionals. The pictures are wonderful, too… and Proverbs come alive in a new way." Her words have encouraged me to encourage others to join me on this spiritual journey.

This guide can be used in three different settings: individual, family, and group. For those who choose to participate, I've included a study guide form that can assist you.

If you decide to take this next step, my suggestion is to read the book of Proverbs first. You may be like me and can't easily absorb much in a short period; so just try to read one chapter each day. There are thirty-one, so it will take about a month.

Then, begin identifying one road sign at a time that interests you. First, view it from a physical standpoint. What is its purpose; why is it in that particular location; what will result if it's ignored; what is its message? Then (this is the important thing) see if you can extract a lesson from it in the context of your spiritual journey. Certainly, you can include some of the signs that I used, but also try to find other ones. And it's fine if your analysis leads you to a different message than mine. Also, try to correlate a lesson gleaned from the sign with one from the book of Proverbs.

When doing this *individually*, you will probably make some of the same discoveries I did. At first, I hardly even noticed the many road signs I routinely passed each day. However, when I chose and then focused on a particular one, a message began to come alive. As I became more familiar with the book of Proverbs, a spiritual light bulb seemed to come that conveyed a deeper, related message. For almost a year, my adventure with road signs served as my devotional, study, and spiritual growth time.

Another interesting, insightful, and fun approach to sign watching is to make it a *family* affair, particularly with young children. Use this as a topic at meals, at bedtime, or in the car on short trips. Have children draw a picture of a sign on the study guide form. Let each one share his or her thoughts and ideas about the sign and especially how it helps on the journey home. Place the drawings on your refrigerator.

I've always enjoyed being a part of a *group* that analyzes and discusses subjects of importance. These include Bible studies, prayer groups, and Sunday school classes. I'm currently in a class that doesn't even have a teacher but instead facilitators. I have learned so much from others who are willing to share experiences and insights concerning their faith journeys. A focused group study on both the physical and spiritual aspects of road signs, coupled with an in-depth exploration of the book of Proverbs, can be a very fruitful and interesting series.

As you can tell from my writings, I'm not the scholarly type. I'm just plain and simple in both my thoughts and activities. So you can understand why something as mundane as road signs caught my eye and sparked my interest. Try it. I think you will discover the same wonder that I did. And your involvement in this exercise may make a difference in your life, as it has in mine.

STUDY GUIDE FORM

(Duplicate and create a page for each sign)
(Draw picture of sign here or on back)

Name of road sign _____
Usual location _____
Purpose of sign (directional, instructional, warning, informational)
_____

Other signs with a similar purpose _____
Message the sign delivers _____
_____

Consequences for violating message _____
_____

Results from adhering to it _____
_____

Spiritual lesson the sign delivers _____
_____
_____

Proverb (chapter and verse) that delivers similar lesson _____
_____
_____

Grandchildren's Road Signs on Refrigerator

OTHER BOOKS BY BERNIE BROWN

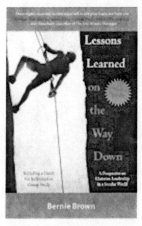

Lessons Learned on the Way Down: A Perspective on Christian Leadership in a Secular World

"These highly readable recollections will touch your heart and help you bridge the gap between your career path and faith journey."

Ken Blanchard,
coauthor of *The One Minute Manager*

Purpose in the Fourth Quarter: Finishing the Game of Life Victoriously

"We all could be well served by adding this little volume to our 'playbooks.'"

Raymond Berry,
NFL wide receiver, head coach, Pro Football Hall of Famer

Snookie and Bernie Are Sweethearts: An Anatomy of a Marriage, coauthored with wife, Snookie

"They make an incredible pair, yielding higher results in their life together than either could have produced alone."

Jenny Brown Bailey, the Browns' firstborn

Visit www.purposeinthefourthquarter.com
Or www.inspiringvoices.com (bookstore)
Bernie's email address: bernielb@bellsouth.net
Snookie's email address: snookierb@bellsouth.net

CPSIA information can be obtained at www.ICGtesting.com
Printed in the USA
LVOW13s0710270314

379061LV00001B/1/P